Basic
Sentence Practice

1-2

Reading and Writing Workbook

Read the sentence

Glue the pictures

Fall Sentence M...

Read

This is my pumpkin craft.

She can put glue on the pumpkin.

Look at all the pumpkin seeds.

Look at that big pump...

Glue

Spring Sentence Matching

Write a sentence for each picture.

Write a sentence

Cut

© A World of L...

Cut out the pictures

Sentences for the whole year!

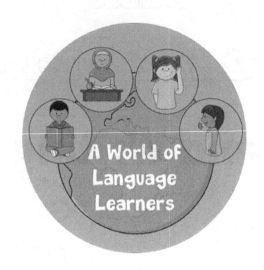

Contact the author :
aworldoflanguagelearners@gmail.com

Table of Contents	Page
Fall	9
Winter	27
Spring	45
Summer	63

Picture Sentence Matching

Have fun practicing reading and writing skills.

First, read the sentences. Then cut out the pictures. Next glue the pictures next to the matching sentence.

On the next page write a sentence for each picture. It can be the same sentence as the one that you glued a picture next to, or you can make up your own sentence.

 Read

He can cut with scissors.	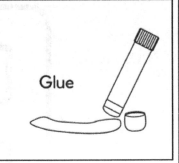 Glue
There is so much food in there.	 Glue
I can see a pencil.	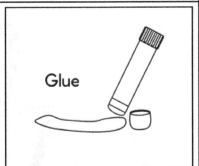 Glue
Look at all the pies.	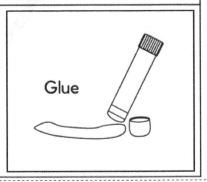 Glue

✂ Cut

Fall Sentence Writing

Write a sentence for each picture.

Read

He has a big pie.

Glue

She has glue.

Glue

The box is full of apples.

Glue

She has a hot drink.

Glue

Cut

Fall Sentence Matching

Write a sentence for each picture.

13

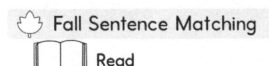

📖 Read

Look at the kids sitting.

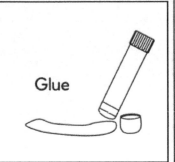
Glue

He has acorns in his bucket.

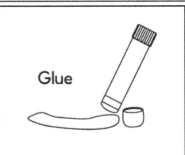
Glue

She is raking the leaves.

Glue

I can see all the sunflowers.

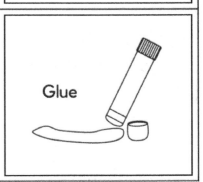
Glue

✂ Cut

 # Fall Sentence Matching

Write a sentence for each picture.

 Read

He has the sunflowers.	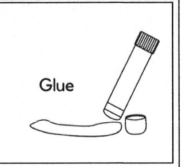 Glue
The kid is playing in the leaves.	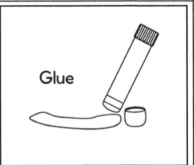 Glue
The leaves come off the tree in fall.	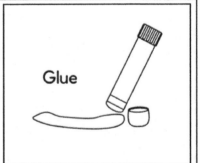 Glue
She has many acorns in her hands.	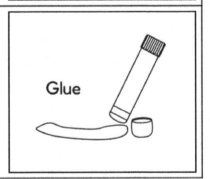 Glue

 Cut

Write a sentence for each picture.

 Read

She can see three pumpkins.

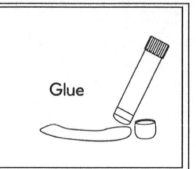
Glue

He can see how tall the pumpkin is.

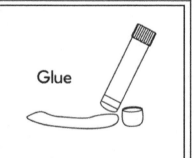
Glue

Look at his pumpkin picture.

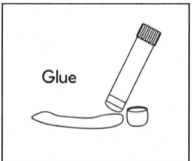
Glue

She can see that the pumpkin is in the water.

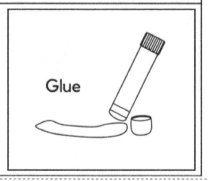
Glue

✂ Cut

Write a sentence for each picture.

 Read

This is my pumpkin craft.

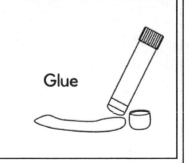
Glue

She can put glue on the pumpkin.

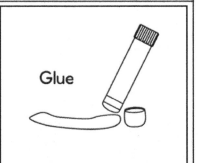
Glue

Look at all the pumpkin seeds.

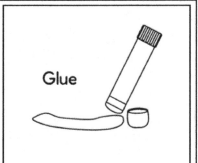
Glue

Look at that big pumpkin.

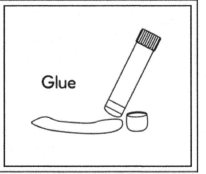
Glue

 Cut

Write a sentence for each picture.

 Read

Look at him glue the apple.

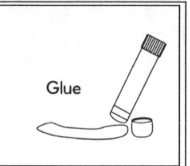
Glue

That tree has five apples.

Glue

The kid can see three apples.

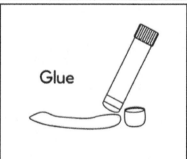
Glue

This apple is in water.

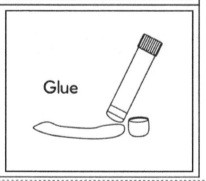
Glue

✂ Cut

Write a sentence for each picture.

 Read

There are many apple seeds here.

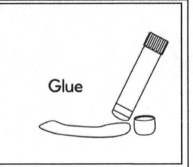
Glue

She has an apple picture.

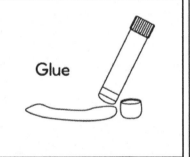
Glue

She can draw an apple.

Glue

A worm is in the apple.

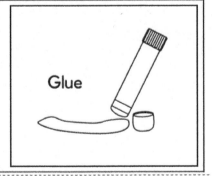
Glue

 Cut

Fall Sentence Matching

Write a sentence for each picture.

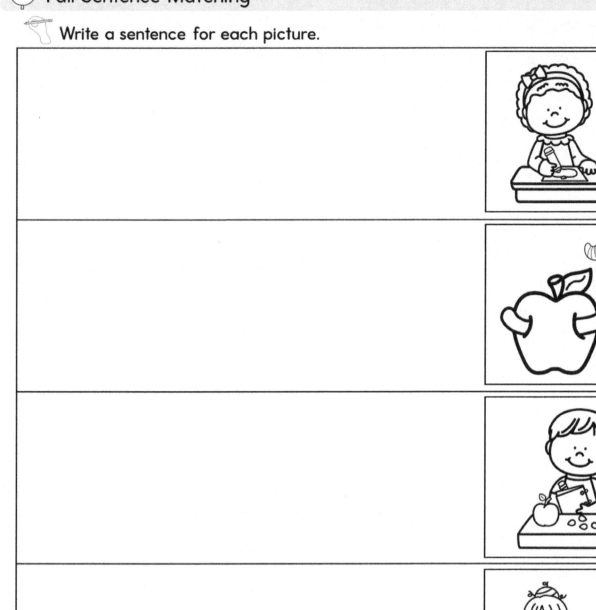

Winter

📖 Read

She has a snowball.

Glue

The bird is in the tree.

Glue

She can mix the pot of soup.

Glue

He is sledding.

Glue

✂ Cut

Winter Sentence Matching

Write a sentence for each picture.

📖 Read

Look at the snow.

Glue

He is skating.

Glue

He is making a snow fort.

Glue

She is cooking.

Glue

✂ Cut

Write a sentence for each picture.

📖 Read

The snowman is melting.

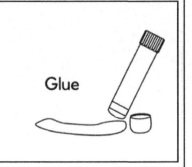
Glue

Look at the mittens.

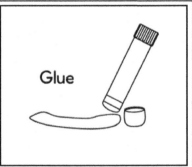
Glue

He can make a snow wall.

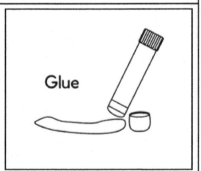
Glue

She is shopping for snacks.

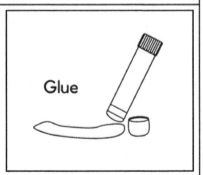
Glue

✂ Cut

Winter Sentence Matching

Write a sentence for each picture.

 **Read**

He can taste the snow.

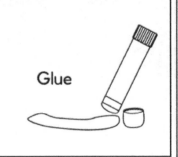
Glue

The bus is full of snow.

Glue

He is making a snowman.

Glue

The kid is looking at the snow.

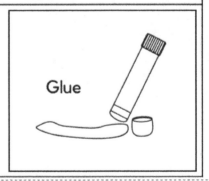
Glue

✂ Cut

Winter Sentence Matching

Write a sentence for each picture.

📖 Read

He has soup.

Glue

She is skating.

Glue

He is putting on his boots.

Glue

He is reading.

Glue

✂ Cut

Winter Sentence Matching

Write a sentence for each picture.

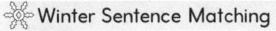
 Read

He is catching the snow.

Glue

The truck can push the snow.

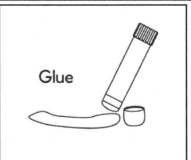
Glue

He has a hot drink.

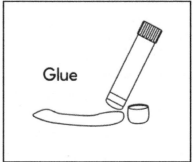
Glue

The car is in the snow.

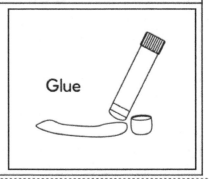
Glue

✂ Cut

Write a sentence for each picture.

📖 Read

Look at the snowball

Glue

Look at that rabbit.

Glue

The cup is hot.

Glue

That house has snow on it.

Glue

✂ Cut

Write a sentence for each picture.

📖 Read

Come and get a hot drink.

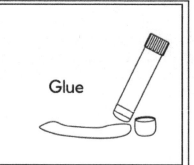
Glue

She is feeding the rabbit.

Glue

She is ice fishing.

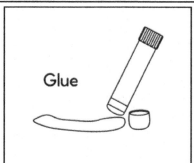
Glue

The fox is in the woods.

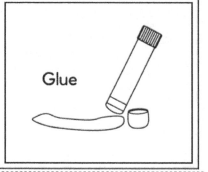
Glue

✂️ Cut

Write a sentence for each picture.

Spring

Read

I have a rain hat.

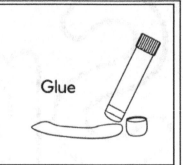

Glue

I can put on my boots.

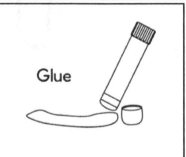

Glue

She can put on her jacket.

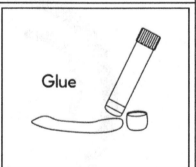

Glue

I like to play in the rain.

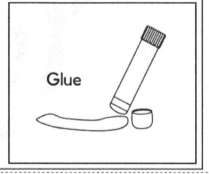

Glue

Cut

🌸 Spring Sentence Matching

Write a sentence for each picture.

 Read

# I can fly a kite.	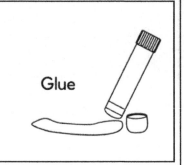 Glue
# Pour the water.	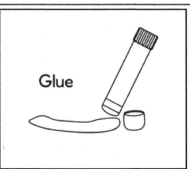 Glue
# It is a windy day.	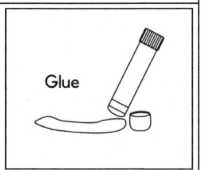 Glue
# Look at all the rain.	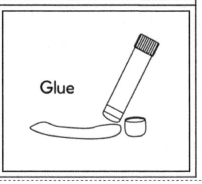 Glue

✂ **Cut**

Spring Sentence Matching

Write a sentence for each picture.

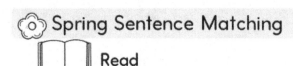
Look at me jump.

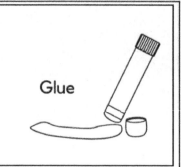
Glue

We like rainbows.

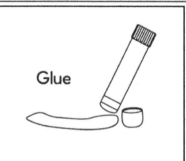
Glue

There are many flowers on the cart.

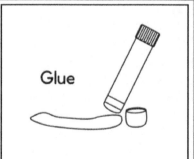
Glue

She has on flowers.

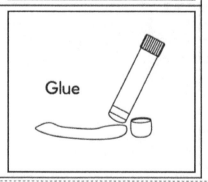
Glue

Cut

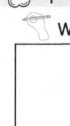

Write a sentence for each picture.

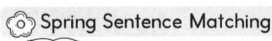

She is looking at the snail.

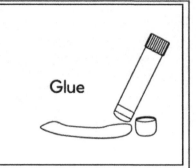

Glue

He has a duck.

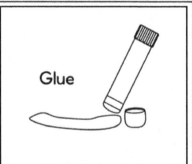

Glue

The snail is on a stick.

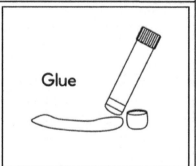

Glue

Look at me splash.

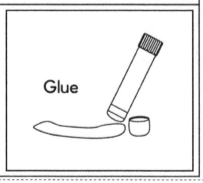

Glue

 Cut

Spring Sentence Matching

Write a sentence for each picture.

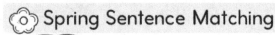

The duck is in the water.  Glue

The frog is on a log. 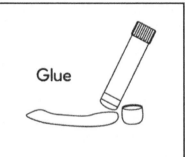 Glue

Watch the flowers grow.  Glue

Look at the bubbles. 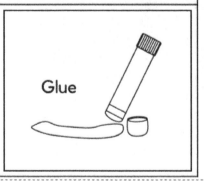 Glue

Cut

Spring Sentence Matching

Write a sentence for each picture.

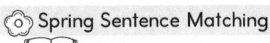
 Read

They are on the swings.

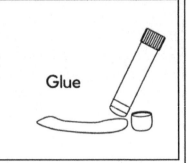
Glue

She can dig.

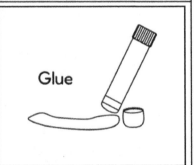
Glue

He can run fast.

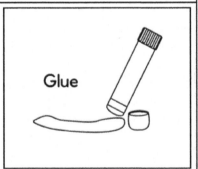
Glue

She is on her bike.

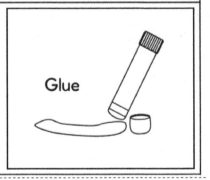
Glue

✂ Cut

Spring Sentence Matching

Write a sentence for each picture.

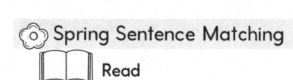

📖 Read

Look at the carrots grow.	Glue 
The bird has a worm.	Glue 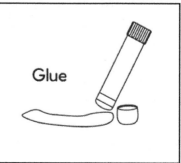
The birds splash in the bird bath.	Glue 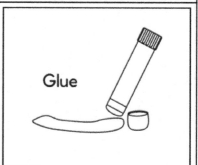
I can plant a tree.	Glue 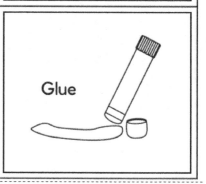

✂ Cut

Write a sentence for each picture.

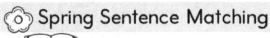
 Read

The seeds go into the hole.	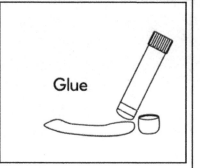 Glue
We like to hike in the woods.	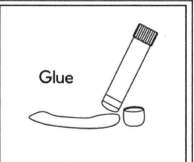 Glue
I can read the map.	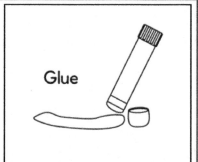 Glue
Look at the boots in the mud.	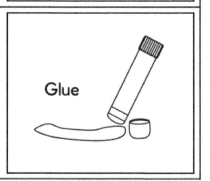 Glue

 Cut

Write a sentence for each picture.

Summer

📖 Read

She is eating.	Glue
They are in the car.	Glue
He can jump.	Glue

She is wet. Glue

✂ Cut

Summer Sentence Matching

Write a sentence for each picture.

📖 Read

Look at them play.

Glue

Look at him eat.

Glue

Where will he go?

Glue

The door is open.

Glue

✂ Cut

Summer Sentence Matching

Write a sentence for each picture.

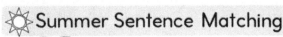

 Read

Look at her play in the sprinkler.	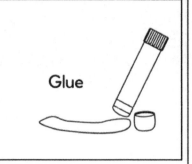 Glue
That is a sandcastle.	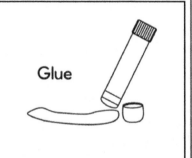 Glue
She can play hopscotch.	 Glue
She has an ice cream cone.	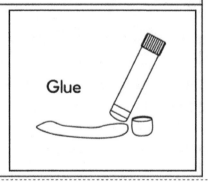 Glue

Cut

 # Summer Sentence Matching

Write a sentence for each picture.

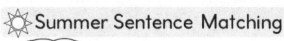

 Read

She will go on a trip.	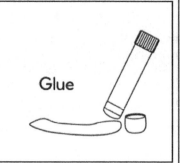 Glue
She is in a tent.	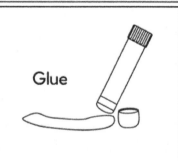 Glue
He is wet.	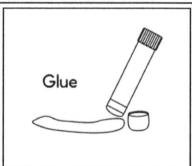 Glue
Look at him put sand into the pail.	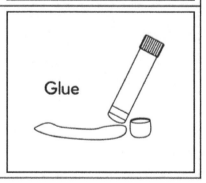 Glue

✂ Cut

Write a sentence for each picture.

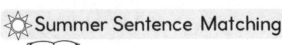

 Read

He is cooking over a fire.	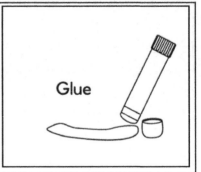 Glue
Do you see that crab?	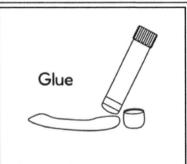 Glue
He can put up the tent.	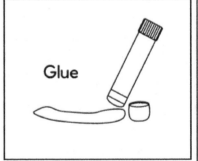 Glue
Look at that ice-cream.	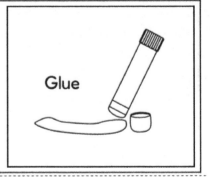 Glue

✂ Cut

Write a sentence for each picture.

📖 Read

Can she get the firefly?

Glue

He can swim with fish.

Glue

He is in a sleeping bag.

Glue

She has lots of shells.

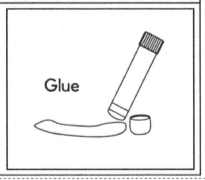
Glue

✂ Cut

Summer Sentence Matching

Write a sentence for each picture.

📖 Read

The kid likes to fish.	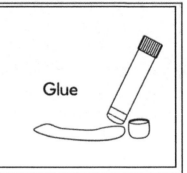 Glue
He can swim fast.	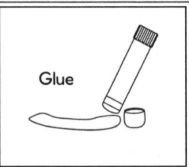 Glue
Look at all the shells.	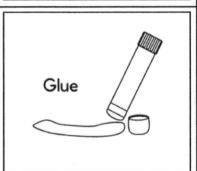 Glue
The fire will cook the snack.	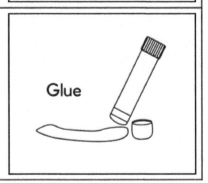 Glue

✂️ Cut

Write a sentence for each picture.

 Summer Sentence Matching

Read

It is a sunny day.	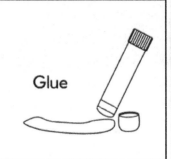 Glue
That is a food stand.	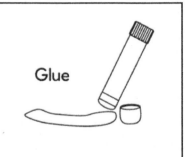 Glue
He can flip the food.	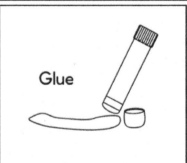 Glue
You can buy a drink.	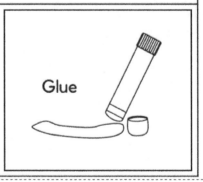 Glue

Cut

Write a sentence for each picture.

Terms of Use

Thank you for purchasing this product.
The contents are the property of Ellie Tiemann and licensed to you only for classroom/personal use as a single user. I retain the copyright, and reserve all rights to this product.

You may not claim this work as your own, giveaway, or sell any portion of this product. You may not share this product anywhere on the internet or on school share sites.

Find more teaching resources at
https://www.teacherspayteachers.com/Store/A-World-Of-Language-Learners

Get weekly tips and find out about teaching resources at
https://www.aworldoflanguagelearners.com/newsletter/

Made in the USA
Coppell, TX
12 November 2024

40078293R00046